Tux Mascot

Tux is a penguin character and the official brand character of the Linux kernel. Originally created as an entry to a Linux logo competition, Tux is the most commonly used icon for Linux, although different Linux distributions depict Tux in various styles. The character is used in many other Linux programs and as a general symbol of Linux.

The concept of the Linux brand character being a penguin came from Linus Torvalds, the creator of Linux. Tux was created by Larry Ewing in 1996 after an initial suggestion made by Alan Cox and further refined by Linus Torvalds on the Linux kernel mailing list. Torvalds took his inspiration from an image he found on an FTP site, showing a penguin figurine looking strangely like the Creature Comforts characters made by Nick Park. The first person to call the penguin "Tux" was James Hughes, who said that it stood for "(T)orvalds (U)ni(X)". However, tux is also an abbreviation of tuxedo, the outfit which often springs to mind when one sees a penguin.

Tux was originally designed as a submission for a Linux logo contest. Three such competitions took place; Tux won none of them. This is why Tux is formally known as the Linux brand character and not the logo. Tux was created by Larry Ewing using the first publicly released version (0.54) of GIMP, a free software graphics package. It was released by him under the following condition:

Permission to use and/or modify this image is granted provided you acknowledge me lewing@isc.tamu.edu and The GIMP if someone asks.

According to Jeff Ayers, Linus Torvalds had a "fixation for flightless, fat waterfowl" and Torvalds claims to have contracted "penguinitis" after being gently nibbled by a penguin: "Penguinitis makes you stay awake at nights just thinking about penguins and feeling great love towards them." Torvalds' supposed illness is a joke, but he claims he was bitten by a little penguin on a visit to the National Zoo & Aquarium, Canberra, Australia. Torvalds was looking for something fun and sympathetic to associate with Linux, and a slightly fat penguin sitting down after having had a great meal perfectly fit the bill.

In an interview Linus commented on the penguin bite:

I've been to Australia several times, these days mostly for Linux.Conf.Au. But my first trip – and the one when I was bitten by a ferocious fairy penguin: you really should keep those things locked up! – was in 93 or so, talking about Linux for the Australian Unix Users Group.

https://en.wikipedia.org/wiki/Tux_(mascot)

Made in the USA
Monee, IL
07 July 2026